Feng Shui for E

Enhance & Harmoniz Business

By

Rob Horrocks

&

Light Wakers

This book is dedicated to our young tribe.

www.lightwakers.com

Acknowledgments

I would like to express my gratitude to the many people who saw me through this book.

I would firstly like to thank my close friends Rick, Eddy, Danny and Tom for their much appreciated support and enthusiasm in all my endeavors; and especially Jay, for he fully understands the ups and downs that we, as Entrepreneurs, go through. Our regular phone calls always provided good enthusiasm, encouragement and chuckles during the ups and downs.

I would especially like to thank my mum (Mercy) and my sister (Rebecca) for the overwhelming support that they have always both provided me with. As well as my closest family, they are both my closet friends too.

Above all I want to thank my partner, soul mate and my best friend Jazmine; who supported and encouraged me in spite of all the time it took me away from her and our young family; the constant long nights, the nonstop computer work and our endless amounts of discussions accompanied by a surplus amount of tea and coffee. It was a long and difficult journey for them all and a journey that couldn't have been completed without them.

Table of Contents

What Is Feng Shui?

Feng Shui (pronounced fung shway) is an ancient Chinese practice that involves art and science. It has been around for thousands of years. The practice relies on the laws of heaven and earth to help people balance their energies within a space. This helps them to bring positivity, fortune and health into their lives.

The word "Feng" means wind and "Shui" means water. Therefore Feng Shui means "wind water". The Chinese people place wind that is gentle and water that is clear into one setting.

Feng Shui prides itself on understanding Chi or Chi energy and the work Chi has to do with energy. Back in ancient times, the Chinese people claimed that the energy of the land would be good for some and bad for others.

Feng Shui comes from the Taoist ideals of dealing with nature. Taoism deals with religious and philosophical beliefs. Taoism has a strong influence all across Asia.

Taoism is also responsible for birthing yin and yang concepts. Yin and yang deal with opposite aspects of a phenomenon or comparing two phenomena. They represent quality in regard to correspondence which is found in most areas of Chinese science and philosophy. An example of this would be ancient Chinese medicine.

In addition to that, the main five Feng Shui elements are also derived from Taoism. When doing a Feng Shui analysis, the Ba-Gua is always used.

The **Ba-Gua** is a grid that is created in a grid of nine sections. Feng Shui Ba-Gua (also called Bagua or Pakua) is one of the main tools used in Feng Shui to analyze the energy of any given space, be it home, office or garden. Basically, Ba-Gua is the Feng Shui energy map of your space that shows you which areas of your home or office are connected to specific areas of your life.

These areas correspond to the most important areas of one's life, the areas that matter the most for one's health and happiness.

*** You can find a large and detailed copy of the Ba-Gua map at the end of this book. ***

The original hexagonal diagram of the Ba-Gua grid has symbols of the I Ching. In fact, Feng Shui is based on this premise. In order for you to connect the areas of your home with Feng Shui, you need to understand the concept of the Ba-Gua map.

風
水

When learning Feng Shui, you have to start off at a basic level in order for you to understand the entire process. After you have a good understanding of Feng Shui at the basic level, you will start to get phenomenal results. The results will affect how you perceive Feng Shui. You will want to use it on a regular basis in your home and in your business.

When engaged with Feng Shui, you will need 'cures' in order to have a better life and to make the most of this art. There are different things that can be used to achieve this. The five most common and important are: aquariums, fountains, crystals, colours and mirrors.

'All the problems we face in our life are closely related to blocked or imbalanced energies in our space, our homes and work places.'

How to use the Ba-Gua Map

Step One - All you need is a basic floor plan of your space. You can simply draw this out as accurately as possible but you don't need to be an architect to do this! A simple layout will do. Using tracing paper often makes it easier to define your home or office Ba-Gua. Then print of a copy of you Ba-Gua map (you can find this at the end of the book).

Step Two - Align the lower end of the Ba-Gua map grid with the wall that has the front door of your home or office space. Now you will have the Ba-Gua map overlaid on top of your home or office space floor plan. The lower part (the bottom row also classed as the North Side) of the Ba-Gua map is always aligned with the wall of the front door, so therefore your front door will be in one of these three Ba-Gua areas:

• Wisdom and Self-Knowledge (North East)

• Career and Life Path (North)

• Helpful People, Spiritual Life and Travel (North West)

Step Three - You can now use the map to help strengthen various areas of your life, such as career, money, relationships and health according to BHS Feng Shui. Begin by familiarizing yourself with each sector of the Ba-Gua and how it relates to the room(s) of your home.

Remember that the compass directions (i.e. North, South, East and West) are related to the Ba-Gua map laid out over you space and not the actual magnetic directions that your space points to with a compass. The central square (the good fortune center) is the heart of your home or office space. Once you know the areas of your home or office that belong to specific areas of your life, you can start applying proper Feng Shui cures and improve the quality of energy in your home.

'Feng Shui is a living skill. There's an art to it. It's scientific; it's mathematical and at times it's logical - with an element of magic thrown in.'

Methods of Feng Shui

Some of the methods are easy to use; however, when it comes to the main part of it, you must dedicate time and patience to understanding and being able to implement this art in the most effective way. Learning Feng Shui is not as easy as people may think it will be, but the rewards far outweigh the cost of leaning this ancient art.

When learning Feng Shui, you should always start from the beginning and with the basics. Only then should you move your way up. This way it'll be it easy for you and others around you to follow and to quickly start feeling the benefits. To get you started, here are some of the things that you can implement:

Air and light of good quality – You should have good air and light in your home in order to master the Feng Shui principles. You will benefit from having good Chi when you incorporate both of them. In order to operate this principle, it's a good idea to allow natural light into your home. The windows should be open on a frequent basis to allow fresh air to circulate. If you're a plant lover, invest in some air purifying plants for your Feng Shui harmonisation.

Ba-Gua – Use the map to activate the energy map in your home. When you connect and use your Ba-Gua map, you will find out which areas or rooms in your home are connected with the Feng Shui concept and how they can be balanced and harmonized.

Five Elements – Get familiar with the five elements of Feng Shui. For certain areas, some elements will need to be stronger. This depends on what you're trying to attract into your life. It also depends on what area of your home you're looking to implement Feng Shui in.

Get Rid of Clutter – You should discard everything that doesn't mean anything to you or reminds you of bad events or feelings in your life. If you have a lot of clutter, all of it can and should be removed as soon as possible. After it's done, you will feel like a heavy burden has been removed from your shoulders. This is a very important thing to do because you will have a release. It will also be easier for you to move on to the next phase.

Birth Element – Wood and fire are considered elements and along with that you will need a colour to correspond with the elements. In addition to that, you will need to incorporate shapes to match the element and colour for Feng Shui.

'A cluttered home/office, leads to a cluttered mind, which in turn leads to a cluttered life.'

The Five Elements of Feng Shui

The five principle elements are important to the concept of Feng Shui. They work in certain ways in accordance with the rotation of the 'productive and destructive cycles'. All five of the elements correspond with a certain colour. Some of the elements will use more than one colour. The best way to utilize these elements is to open your space to more positivity and happiness.

Here are the five elements and their corresponding colours:

- **Wood** – Represents and provides energy for health and vitality; it also represents abundance and is considered a cure for wealth and prosperity. This element resides in the East and Southeast areas of your space. The Wood Element is also good for use in the South. The Wood Element colours are brown and green.

- **Fire** – Represents high energy and passion and it provides energy to things that are career related. It will also provide assistance to have you recognized in your achievements. This element resides in the South, Northeast and Southwest areas of your space. The Fire Element colours are Red, Orange, Purple, Pink and Strong Yellow.

- **Water** – Represents easiness, abundance and freshness; it also represents calm and purity. Water represents abundance and is considered a cure for Feng Shui. It can be used in the North, East and Southeast areas of your space. The Water Element colours are blue and black.

- **Earth** – Represents being stable and nourished; it also represents protection for your relationships. It can be used in the Northeast, Southeast and Center areas of your space. The Earth Element colours are beige and yellow.

- **Metal** – Represents being precise and clear; it also represents exactness and being efficient. It helps you to live with clarity and light. It can be used in the West, North and Northwest areas of your space. The Metal Element is ideal for your home or business. The Metal Element colours are white and gray.

風
水

The productive and destructive cycles control the five elements of Feng Shui. Wood is part of the productive cycle that is produced by the Element Water. The cycle continues with the creation of Fire, Earth, Metal and last but not least Water. They should always be in that order and constantly cycling. The cycle does not stop and they maintain their positive and consistent flow with one another.

Even though it's on the opposite end, the destructive cycle has just as much prominence as the productive cycle. Anything that is negative or contributes to decay is removed. This makes way for things that are positive and will help in the harmonizing Feng Shui process.

With this cycle, Wood is responsible for separating Earth. Earth in turn, soaks up Water; Water douses out Fire; Fire melts Metal; and Metal cuts up Wood. This too, is another cycle that goes around in circles and does not stop.

You will need to use different colours for each direction:

- East and Southeast – Dominant green

- South – Dominant red

- Southwest – Dominant yellow

- West and Northwest – Dominant white or metallic

With the directions and colour schemes, alternate colours can be used for the basic ones. Blue and black can be used for the East and Southeast. Anything in the red family can be used for the Southwest and Northwest.

Anything in the yellow, beige and brown family along with any combinations can be used for the West and Northwest. White is the colour used in the North because Metal creates Water. In the South, green can be used because Wood creates Fire.

The colours don't have to stand by themselves. They can be supplemented or combined with others to create powerful statements. With Feng Shui, you must keep balance and harmony. These attributes are needed in order to keep the flow of Chi in a positive format.

Yang energy comes from the Element of Fire. It is represented by the colour red. Other things that help to provide more of this energy are candles and lights. If you want more intimacy in your relationship, Earth energy would be needed. Things that contribute to earth energy can help your marriage or partnered relationship in a positive way. They can also help you in different relationships of a loving but none intimate way.

You can use things like crystals and ceramics, things made from earthenware to enhance this. Since Metal is created by Earth, Metal can take advantage of the benefits from Earth. Metal is also one of the Yang Elements that happens to have a positive effect of relationships. Metal is also responsible for creating Water. This can help with the Chi flow too.

With Water being a part of the Chi flow, the flow doesn't stop. Water helps to have Chi flowing into different areas of your life. With Feng Shui, flowing water is considered to very balancing and will provide with a quiet and relaxing atmosphere. You can also use it to implement energy in your home.

風
水

If you are looking to advance or start your career, water can be used for that purpose. It also represents wealth and prosperity. A good thing to implement for this would be an aquarium or a water fountain. This can have positive vibes in certain areas of your home. One place that water is not recommended for is the bedroom.

The Wood Element also connects with your home and garden. You can place wooden objects in certain areas in order to obtain more wealth. They can be placed near plants and flowers. Another thing that can increase wealth is installing a wooden bench in the area of your garden that is designated for Wealth.

"No one saves us but ourselves. No one can and no one may. We ourselves must walk the path." – Buddha

The Colours of Feng Shui

- **Black**

Black is the colour of mystery. It also provides protection. It symbolizes nighttime, when it gets dark, and it also represents an empty space. Even with that, it provides intensity to any area. If it is used often, it can translate into a heavy atmosphere. Black is also used to provide strength.

This color can be used in the East, North and Southeast. It should not be used in the South. It can be used in a child's bedroom, but not a lot. It can also be used in the common areas of your home.

If you're trying to attract career opportunities, it can be used in the North area of anyone's space. Black can be combined with white to be used on furniture too.

- **Brown**

The colour brown is used in the East, Southeast and the South. The energy from this colour provides plenty of nourishment. It can be associated with different foods and drinks, such as chocolate and coffee as well.

Brown can also be used for the common areas of your home. You shouldn't use much of the colour Brown for a child's bedroom or in the Southwest area. If there is too much of the colour in an area, it may cause people not to take a step forward.

- **Green**

This colour represents revival and a fresh start. Green provides nourishment and keeps peace in your life. When incorporated with Feng Shui, you should use different versions of green, instead of just one. You can use plants that have fresh foliage to enhance and bring this colour into your life. Green is also known to provide healing. It can be used in the South, East and Southeast areas.

- **Purple**

Don't overuse the colour purple. This colour is very strong, and has a relationship with the spirit. It is not recommended for use on any walls. It can however, be used in a space where meditation is taking place. If you use this colour at home, be very moderate about using it. You can use lighter colour variations of it, but always in moderation. It can be used in the East South and West areas, nut again always with limitations. A good way for the colour purple to be implemented is to use the Feng Shui crystal Amethyst.

- **Red**

When the colours for Feng Shui are used in the right format, your environment will be the recipient of good Feng Shui energy. The colour red contributes to the Fire Element to provide energy.

Fire can be considered as a creative aspect and a destructive aspect too. Fire is a symbol for the sun, life and the energy that comes from life. With this Element in your home, you can experience happiness and a desire to be sexually fulfilled.

Red also represents passion and celebration. The Chinese use the colour red for happiness and luck. In India, the colour red is use for marriage and weddings, and in the West, the colour red stands for romance and courage.

When people decorate, the colour red is used for richness. Careful consideration has to be implemented so as not to use too much red. Otherwise, it can provoke anger and excessive stimulation.

With Feng Shui, red can be used in children's bedrooms with caution. It can also be used in the common areas of the home, such as the dining rooms, living rooms and the kitchen area.

In the East, Southeast, West and Northwest areas of your home, you can use the colour red, but you are limited to how much you should use. Red is a perfect candidate to use in the South.

- **Orange**

Orange has been nicknamed the "social" colour. Orange is responsible for providing the energy from Feng Shui to engage in spirited conversations and to have good feelings in your home. When the winter season approaches, it can be a reminder of the summer season. Log fires also come into play with the color of orange.

Just like red represents fire, so does orange. It is not a good colour for the areas of the West and Northwest. In addition to that, this colour should not be seen in the East and

Southeast. These areas are controlled by other elements of Feng Shui.

Orange can be used in the common areas, such as the living and dining rooms, kitchen and anywhere else where the environment has lots of action and lots of energy. It's a good idea to have some Feng Shui products or accessories to accompany this colour.

Since orange is considered a soft and warm color, it is easy to incorporate with Feng Shui. It is a beautiful sight to see, just like watching a sunset is beautiful. It enhances the rooms and makes them stand out too.

• **Pink**

The colour of love is pink. It can also be used to keep the energy calm. It also works to quiet the heart and provide it with lots of love. This colour is used mostly in the Southwest area. It is also in line with marriage. When decorating, a soft pink is usually used. When there is hot and heavy energy, hot or vibrant pink is used.

Pink is great to use for a bedroom of a young child, as the loving energy that a young child craves can be found in the energy of this colour. There are several common combinations of pink that work well, including pink and black and pink and green. With Feng Shui, Rose Quartz crystals can be used for love. The crystals are a soft pink colour that soothes the soul. The vibrational energy from this crystal is always very powerful as well.

- **Yellow**

The colour yellow reminds people of the sun. It can brighten up any space and provides an inviting atmosphere. You have many choices to choose from when it comes to yellow. This colour is a really good choice for a child's bedroom and the family room.

If you have a dull looking room, using the colour yellow will provide it with lots of light. It provides the Fire Element, but in a softer format than the color Red does. It is easier to deal with on a larger scale too. Yellow can also be used to provide self-esteem. If you use hot yellow, don't use too much of it. Yellow can be used in the East and Southeast areas.

- **Gray**

Gray is usually considered as a dull colour that doesn't have much life. However, there is a shade of gray (noble gray) that is considered a little more upbeat than the regular color. Gray is used in the West, Northwest and North areas of Ba-Gua.

It should not be used too much in the East and Southeast. Wood is the dominant Element in those areas. Believe it or not, gray can provide Feng Shui energy into most of the common areas in your home as well.

It can provide a clear focus to any space in your home. Gray also represents the energy of the Metal Element.

- **White**

The colour white represents Yoga rituals. With Feng Shui, it stands for quietness and innocence. It also stands for beginnings and endings. It has a clean and fresh focus. It can be used for Feng Shui purposes anywhere in your home.

In the East and Southeast, it's not a good idea to use just white though. You can use other colours to blend in with it or to enhance the area.

You can have white space in your bathroom or mediation room. This will help with healing in your home. It can also provide possibilities never explored before along with a promising future.

- **Blue**

Blue represents the clear skies and waters. It can be used in the East and Southeast of anyone's space. Since blue is connected with Water, the energy that is responsible for supplying nourishment to the Wood Element. It can also be use for decoration or art. Blue can also be used as a colour for ceilings. It's been noted that students did better in their studies when they had a blue ceiling.

For harmony, a light blue colour would work well. For peace and quiet, a dark blue colour would work better. A deep blue colour can be implemented into your bedroom to help to get to sleep. For the South, West and Northwest areas, deep blue should not be utilized much. Blue and white colours can be combined to provide a really balanced energy.

'The space in which we live should be for the person we are becoming now, not for the person we were in the past.'

Creating a Happy Home with Feng Shui

The areas that are incorporated with Feng Shui are built to have energy in mind. There is always energy around us that continues to circulate every minute of every day. You can do the same thing at your home. Incorporating the principles of Feng Shui can help you to have a healthy and happy home.

When you do this, expect the atmosphere to change. When people come to visit, they will feel happier to be in your home and in your presence. When they are happy, you will be happy. If you were pessimistic before, your demeanor will change to the opposite. As long as you keep the exchange of positive energy flowing, you will be able to relish in any type of environment.

Get familiar with certain areas of your home. The more you are aware about what the areas are comprised of, the more success you will have of incorporating those areas with the principles of Feng Shui. With this, you will be able to transfer this to other areas of your life, including your relationships with family members and friends.

Let's look at some things that can advance and enhance this:

- You should have a connection to your home. Examine the areas of your home and determine which parts do not line up with the Feng Shui principles. Whatever doesn't line up will eventually have a detrimental effect in your life. It will also cause you not to have as much energy in those areas.

- Don't overreact if your home or areas are not responding the way you would like them to. An example would be if you have a basement in your home that is in need of painting. Don't get upset because it hasn't been painted. Everything will flow into place. Just stay positive and keep moving forward in a positive direction.

- Create Feng Shui instructions for yourself so that you can move forward, step by step and get the work done. Don't get angry or agitated as you list what needs changing. Just think of it as a map of steps in the right direction. There will be time when you can let out your emotions, but don't allow them to be a hindrance with this assignment.

風
水

- Remove as much of the clutter from your home. When you remove clutter from your home, you are able to provide positive and fresh energy. Your home will also be healthier as a result. Having clutter represents confusion and indecisiveness, which can prove to be a negative thing for you if you're working to incorporate Feng Shui in your life. Once the clutter is gone, you will have a sense of relief and whatever stress you had will be gone. This can also help you to have a healthier peace of mind.

Another thing that some people feel they are lacking in is relationships, whether it's a marriage, friendship, or relationship with your children, siblings, parents or other relatives. How does this work in the equation? Well, having positive relationships can provide you with more energy and a more positive life.

People want to feel that someone cares about their well-being. Maintaining any kind of relationship takes work and it doesn't happen overnight. There are some that are healthy, and others are just falling by the wayside.

In regard to your home, there are some ways that can help you to keep your relationships fresh and positive:

- Change the format of your furniture. If you have enough room, move it around to another angle or another wall. Don't keep any furniture, such as a sofa, bed, table or chairs in the same format every year. It starts to become monotonous. Moving your furniture around regularly can help provide more energy in that area.

- Whatever area of your house it is, focus on providing additional energy that is positive. You can do that by having fresh fruit, fresh flowers, or anything that is fresh, vibrant and stands out.

- Your bedrooms, bathrooms and even your storage cupboards/closets should all be clutter free. They should be areas that people wouldn't mind looking at if you were showing them your house.

- Having pictures of you and your loved ones in a positive format is a great thing to bring into your space.

- Don't crowd people and don't allow them to crowd you. Everyone needs space and time for themselves, so make sure that everyone in your home has this in their lives. Remember, your home is also your sanctuary.

- Remember that positive thoughts create positive things.

- Remove that TV from your bedroom.

Having a television in your bedroom is never usually a good idea. It can be a distraction from your actual purpose. A lot of people won't like to hear that, but the TV, although it can be used for relaxation, it is a source of negative energy and best kept for the living room. Also, on that note, I would just like to add that falling asleep with the TV on can be very bad for your health. Especially if what you are subconsciously listening to is negatively based. While you sleep, your subconscious will pick up all of the energy that you are listening too!

'You should sit and meditate for twenty minutes every day – unless you're too busy; then you should sit and mediate for an hour.' – Ancient Zen Adage

Feng Shui if Your Home is in a Cul-de-sac

Feng Shui needs more effort and energy put into it when your home is located in a cul-de-sac. Here are some explanations as to why a cul-de-sac home may not receive the proper flow of Feng Shui that it should and why the extra effort and focus needs to be given. When a home is in a cul-de-sac, there is a back and forth movement of shared energy between homes of three or more. The energy within those homes wavers and can't be still. This causes less energy to flow through; of course, this hinges on the homes in that particular cul-de-sac. If you are surrounded by negative homes, then a lot of the surround energy will be negative. The opposite is true if the homes surround yours are positively focused.

Here are some ways that the Feng Shui cul-de-sac issue can be solved:

- The landscaping should be neat and provide a good, flow of energy. The homes should also have a quality backing that is sturdy and will hold up. Evergreens can also be installed in the back of the home to aid this.

- The walkway to the front of the home should be curved rather than straight. This brings a more natural flow into the front of your home. Also in the front of the home, plant some greens and decorate the area with colorful rocks. At least the person coming to visit will have something positive and balancing to look at as they come to the front of your home.

- If possible, install a fountain or moving water feature outside the front of your home. Or you could install a birdbath. With Feng Shui, the fountain or birdbath should be installed in the direction that your home is facing. In addition to that, the water flow should be flowing in the same direction as well.

- Your front door may need to be a certain colour too. If your door is facing North, you may want to opt for a black or blue colour for the door. Since that represents calm and will lessen confusion in and around your home.

Just remember that each home is different, so there may be some homes within a particular cul-de-sac that may have plenty of positive energy to aid Feng Shui. There may be some outside of that area that do not have that energy. There are several factors that play into this scenario so just do your best and know that you are focused on the positive energy around you.

Why You Should Not Use Direct Alignment for the Doors in Your Home

When using Feng Shui, it's important that the doors directly opposite other doors are covered or closed if possible. This is important, if not more important than the rest of the spaces in the home. Direct alignment of more than one door is not proper, it doesn't aid in the positive energy flow and it can contribute to bad Feng Shui.

Even though the concept of Feng Shui is to have a balance with the energy flow in your home, having a direct alignment with more than one door cannot work. The quality of energy flow from Feng Shui is subject to decrease. One area where you do not want to do this is with the front and the back door. The majority of the energy from the good Feng Shui is brought in through the front door. If those two doors are aligned, the energy can travel through the back door. This is not good because the energy from the good Feng Shui needs to permeate throughout your home, not just entering and leaving straight away.

Take note of what kind of energy is being created in your home. If it's not enough, see what you can do to create more positive energy for Feng Shui. However, if you do have doors in your home that are directly aligned with each other, there are some things that you can do to remedy the situation:

- In order for you to change the energy due to the way the doors are situated, you may have to change the colour of one of the doors. After the colour change, the relationship will be different and one of the doors will have more strength than the other.

- Where the energy is, you can place a small round table there. The energy will be directed elsewhere and the energy will slow down. For improvement, add a vase or similar container with fresh flowers. Doing this will give more credence to the energy.

- If you don't want to use fresh flowers, get a plant to send the energy in another direction.

The purpose in doing these things is to redirect the energy in another direction. Don't forget to incorporate Chi and send the water flow in another direction too. It's important to keep the energy from Feng Shui flowing in and around your home.

Feng Shui for Your Kitchen

Incorporating Feng Shui for your kitchen will take some focus and thought. You have to look at how it is placed within the home. The kitchen is usually located adjacent to the rear of the home. There's a good reason for that.

From a visual standpoint, if the kitchen was near or at the front, it could pose a mindset of issues with eating and nutrition. Having the kitchen at the front of the home could mean that you may be tempted to eat every time you enter. It would be just as bad if you have guests coming to visit. The first thing they would subconsciously want to do is eat!

However, if your home is set up like this, you can do something about it. You could purchase a curtain or subtle partition and install in at the doorway or entry point of the kitchen. Or, you could have French doors measured to be installed there. Another idea you could implement is to have something that will peak their interest to divert attention away from the kitchen.

If you're cooking, you should have an eye on the entrance to the kitchen while cooking. This is usually somewhat difficult however because most kitchens have the stove or oven against a wall. To implement to the Feng Shui method, people that are cooking can put a mirror over the stove to allow focus on the other parts of the kitchen and especially the entrance.

For newer homes, builders are now including islands that sit in the middle of the kitchen area. This is a good addition to the Feng Shui concept. When the island is strategically placed in the middle, the person that's cooking can see what's going on in other areas.

When it's set up this way, they can still be involved with what's happening in a nearby area, along with continuing to cook.

This type of kitchen setup is inviting because it allows other people to come in and help cook without getting in each other's way. The flow of energy can move around. The original person that was doing all of the cooking won't feel trapped. It can also make for a greater camaraderie and relationship bonding.

In Feng Shui, the stove or oven is the symbol of health and wealth. All of the burners should be used equally by doing rotations. Don't use one or two burners and leave the rest unused. Using all four in equal rotation can cause you to receive money from more than one source. Most people tend to have their 'favorite' burner, that they always seem to use and they don't really know why. Change this habit!

While microwaving food may be quick and convenient, in the interim you may feel rushed. People that faithfully practice the Feng Shui method do not like to use microwaves due to lots of radiation and the bad energy that this causes.

The kitchen should be one of the cleanest areas in the home. It should also be completely clutter-free. If you have anything that is not working properly or not working at all, it should be discarded at once. Having something that doesn't work or doesn't work properly defeats the purpose and the principles of Feng Shui.

You can also use different design methods and patterns from the Feng Shui concept. The methods most used are a shaker style concept - contemporary with solid colours and wood grains and a wealthy look - that comes with carvings and other related items.

The kitchen should have adequate lighting and use different types. There should be enough space to move around. The more space you have, the better. If it means you have to move machines and appliances to create more space, then so be it.

You don't need a lot of kitchen equipment or utensils in front of you. Use only the things that you're going to cook with. When you're finished with those items, you can place them in the sink to be washed later. At least they will be out of the way.

To increase the energy in the kitchen, you may want to have some fruit, flowers or plants on the table. This will also brighten up the kitchen to make it look more inviting. Cooking in the kitchen is where the heart is. You want to have a place where people can come and enjoy your company and of course, your tasty food!

'Quiet the mind and then the soul will speak.'

Create Wealth and Abundance Using Feng Shui in Your Bathroom

A bathroom is one of the places where you can incorporation Feng Shui for the purpose of wealth. There are different strategies that you can use to accomplish this.

- **Colour** – From the different elements, you can use different colours to achieve your goal of attracting wealth from using Feng Shui. With Wood, you should use brown and green; with Water, use blue and black; with Earth, use light yellow or light beige.

- **Crystals** – You can purchase Feng Shui or energy crystals to use. Mix them up using amethyst, citrine, rose quartz and others in the crystal family. This combination can create a wealth cure in Feng Shui.

- **Bamboo** – Another Feng Shui cure for wealth and abundance is to have 8 stalks of Lucky Bamboo. This cure is used by a lot of people and they can be found in plenty of floral retailers. All five elements of Feng Shui have a part to play in the Bamboo plant.

- **Atmosphere** – Decorate your bathroom so that it looks like a relaxing and inviting spa. A spa is a place where you go to relax. All you should be thinking about in this space is having a peace and relaxation.

- **Clutter** – Remove any excess or clutter that doesn't need to be there. If you have items that have expired, get rid of them. If there are things that you haven't used in a long time, get rid of those too. You want to have things in your bathroom that represent positive energy, not old and empty things. It's also important that the lighting is good as well.

- **Meaning of wealth** – Whatever wealth means to you, put something that represents it in the bathroom. It could be a picture, a poem or some quote that will remind you of wealth.

- **Toilet seat** – The toilet seat should remain down when not in use. This, apart from being simply polite and of good manners, will show that the energy will be maintained and will not spread out everywhere outside of that area.

Mirrors with Feng Shui

Mirrors are generally used as a reflection. People use them to look themselves. With Feng Shui, they help to bring in water. They are also used to pull in the Chi method in addition to widening space. Mirrors can change the way energy flows in a certain area. They are good for bringing peace and a fresh new outlook on life.

With Feng Shui there are four types of mirrors are to consider. Here's a brief synopsis of them:

- **Convex** – These mirrors are considered to represent protection. They are the eyes and ears and most of the time, are utilized apart from Feng Shui. They can also be used within the concept, but they have to be framed in a certain way.

- **Concave** – Most of the time, these mirrors are not used with Feng Shui. The reflection from the mirrors is a smaller version that is turned upside-down. This is not a good reflection.

- **Typical** – Depending on the shape and the frame, it represents a certain Feng Shui cure. They are usually placed in the Southwest portion of your areas.

- **Ba-Gua Mirror**, which is separate from the three mirrors mentioned above. It is very powerful and for the most part, people don't use it correctly. It is only made for outdoors, not indoors. If you're not feeling the right kind of energy in your home or business, then this type of mirror will come in handy for you. This mirror is not to be used for decoration as it's energy is very powerful and should not be taken for granted.

The Ba-Gua mirror is found in concave and convex formats. The Ba-Gua itself is made from wood and there is usually a choice of green, red or gold. The Ba-Gua mirror is good to use if you need to protect yourself from harm or danger, such as attacks against you or if there are people out to harm you. You should consult with a person that is knowledgeable in Feng Shui to make sure that it is placed in the right area. Most times, it is placed above the main entrance to your home. One place that it should not ever be placed at is in the living room, if it does ever enter the home.

Feng Shui in Your Bedroom to Enhance Your Love Life

In order to have a positive, intimate relationship with your partner, you need a good Feng Shui bedroom. Both of you will be able to spend time renewing yourselves, minus having to deal with a lot of unnecessary stuff.

Only one significant piece of furniture should be placed in your bedroom and that's the bed. You have to have something to sleep on! Get something simple like a wooden bed frame along with a natural mattress. The sheets that you sleep under should be made from cotton of the best quality or close. Do not have any electronics except things like a clock.

Part of the Yin culture includes sleeping. It is important that the bedroom is situated at the back of your home where there is minimal activity. Your bedroom should look warm and inviting. After all, it is where you share intimate and tender moments alone with each other.

Here are some more Feng Shui suggestions you can use for your bedroom:

- The bedroom should not be placed over a garage. This is where you can incorporate low energy and issues with your health. Also, electrical elements from the vehicle parked in the garage can mess with your electromagnetic system.

- Try not to use items that run on electricity in the bedroom. These items can provoke a high electrical charge and negative energy.

- If possible, the bedroom should not be anywhere near the kitchen, bathroom, living room or children's bedroom.

- To keep the flames going in your sex and love life, there should always be fresh energy in the bedroom. This can be implemented by using crystals, candles or essential oils.

Keeping the bedroom with good Feng Shui will help to maintain a positive flow and sensual feelings of energy. A good Feng Shui bedroom should be filled with lots of love and passion. It should also be exciting and provide relaxation.

'Space equals grace.'

Here are some more ways that you can create a good Feng Shui bedroom:

- Don't have stale air in your bedroom. Open the window and let in some fresh air, weather permitting. You should have fresh air flowing in your bedroom. In addition to removing the majority of electrical appliances, it is not advisable to have plants in the bedroom, either.

- The lighting in the bedroom should be adjustable. The easiest way to do this is to install a dimmer switch. You will be able to adjust the lights to an appropriate level. You can also use candles, but purchase those that are toxin free.

- Use colours that correspond with the Feng Shui method. The colours should create a balance for the bedroom. This way, you will be assured of a positive energy flow. This will help you go to sleep better. It will also help your sexual life as well. Some colours that work well include whites and chocolate brown colours.

- If you're looking to add art to your bedroom, choose pieces that reflect how you look at your life and your future in a positive way. Refrain from using pieces that represent anything that is the opposite of that.

The Feng Shui procedure for your bed should be as follows:

- You should be able to gain access to your bed from both sides. The bed should not be parallel with the bedroom door. You can have two small tables on each side of your bed. Doing these things will help your bed and bedroom maintain a balance.

- All of the doors that are connected to the bedroom should be closed. This will keep the energy flow inside of the bedroom. It will also enhance your relationship with your partner.

You want to have a bedroom that will be the symbol of pleasure, intimacy and love. Using the Feng Shui method can help you do just that.

Feng Shui for Your Home Based Business

Believe it or not, there are many business people all over the world that use the principles of Feng Shui in their business. Many people believe Feng Shui is necessary in order to conduct proper business and business management. In fact, there are some very famous business people all over the world that are using Feng Shui and they have encountered good success in their businesses as well as their personal lives.

Many people have transformed themselves into entrepreneurs and having their office established in their home. This is a cost effective way to start out because it keeps your overheads low.

On the other side, some people that work from home find themselves somewhat perplexed because it can be difficult for them to separate their home business from their personal life and also they don't have a lot of interaction with other people. However, having a home based business outweighs the challenges and frustrations that people face when working 9 to 5 jobs.

If you're looking to attract wealth and abundance for your home based business using Feng Shui, here are some ways to incorporate it:

- You should always sit with a solid wall behind your back. Avoid sitting with a window behind you.

- You should not have a wall facing you while you're at your desk working.

- Wherever your wealth area is on your map, you should have the office equipment placed there.

- In order for Chi to flow with harmony, place the tables and chairs in a strategic format.

- Have air-purifying plants in your office. This will help supply you with a fresh quality of air and it will also increase the amount of oxygen generated in that area.

- Other than air-purifying plants, refrain from having any plants that have sharp edges, such as cactus.

- The entry door to your office should be free of obstruction. If there is obstruction, such as a table behind the door, the Chi will not operate correctly and to it's full ability.

- In order to enhance the presence of Chi, a good idea is to install a hanging crystal in your office.

- Your office should be a good distance from your bedroom, if you have a home based office.

- Your office should be about productivity. The colours of your office should reflect that.

- The copy machine or printer should not be near the main entrance door. The heat from the copy machine can cause Chi not to flow correctly.

There are different areas of your office that need to be nurtured with Feng Shui. In the North area, the Water Element is used as well as Metal. In your office, it's fine to have images with black or white frames.

- If there is an empty vase near the main entry door, the Chi will find its way into the empty vase. This will be detrimental to the environment.

- If you have clients that come to see you, try placing a fish tank within the wealth area. This will help you get better results and probably more clients, which in turn, means more money. You have to be careful to follow the instructions for doing this; otherwise it won't work, so spend some time researching this further.

- In order to get Chi working properly, install a small indoor fountain in your wealth corner. This method will also help you health wise.

- Keep your desks and surrounding areas clutter free. To help with this, do not use paper trays.

- Pay attention to the kind of light that you are using in your home office. You should use both natural and artificial lighting. You will not be able to function properly if you don't have enough natural light. You should also think about getting other type of lights, such as full-spectrum lights.

There are different areas of your office that need to be nurtured with Feng Shui. In the North area, the Water Element is used as well as Metal. In your office, it's fine to have images with black or white frames.

The South area uses Fire for energy. You should refrain from having blue mirrors, or images of water or anything that represents this colour. The Southeast area is for images that represent prosperity and abundance. The Wood Element is best used here. With this, you should refrain from Fire and Metal images.

Using these Feng Shui principles will help your business to thrive and grow in prosperity and abundance.

'Clutter is not just physical stuff. It's old ideas, toxic relationships and bad habits. Clutter is anything that does not support you better self.'

Using Feng Shui for Your Internet Business

You can use Feng Shui to create harmony for your websites. Your web pages must be aligned properly. You want the visitors that come to your site to have easy navigation and access. It should be a positive experience for them. The pages should be clean and use bright colours for the background. If you create web pages with dark colours, it can be a turn off to those that are visiting your website. In order to start to Chi flowing, you can use bold and vibrant colours.

White and blue are a few that come to mind. These colours are the symbols of air and water. If you use colours that don't blend very well, your website will not be very attractive.

Refrain from adding things like animated graphics (if possible) that take away from the essence of the website. If it has to be part of the website, then make sure that it's something that looks natural.

On your website, you should have an area that displays a logo. This logo would be on every webpage that you create. Refrain from putting a lot of games and other gimmicks on your website and web pages. This will distract the visitors.

Your website should have a main menu page. All of the elements that you're putting on the website should be neatly lined up on one side of the screen not cluttered on both sides of the screen.

Don't make your website look so professional that no one will want to stay. Create websites that will bring harmony and good atmosphere to the visitors. If you're going to incorporate music, use music that is relaxing. This will help to create positive Chi.

The important thing with creating websites using Feng Shui is that you want them to be simple, easy to navigate and not look rushed or cluttered. Too much information on it and people will turn away in a heartbeat.

Ironically, having a rushed or cluttered website can be reflective of the person themselves. It's all about having a positive flow so that good Chi will continue to flow through.

Using Feng Shui for a Retail Business

You may want to open up a retail shop, maybe you have one already or maybe you are in charge of running a shop. Having plenty of products, but not having any idea on how to attract or keep customers once they set foot in your business can be a major problem. Here we'll help you to understand what's going on and provide some assistance in this area. Using the principles of Feng Shui can change your situation. Here's a look at some things that you can do to change the atmosphere of your business:

- Don't keep too many things bunched together. Products are nice, but keep a sense of organisation and what goes where.

- You must remove some of the products and leave some space between them. Bunching them up together does nothing but cause confusion for the customer. They feel it's too much for them to look at. Space equals grace.

- Try to put the products in specific categories. Then you'll see a difference when customers come in. They'll want to stay longer and look because they're not confused and frustrated with what to purchase.

- The Feng Shui energy from the front door to the back door must flow properly. If not, you won't get customers or sales. The minute the customer walks in the door, they need to be drawn in by your energy and the energy of your place.

- The entrance and the front area should be more visible than the back. They will see the front of the store first before they make their way back. So this should make sense.

- If your aisles are not clear and you have things in the way that are creating obstacles for the customer, this will create bad energy. A customer doesn't want to be squeezing through or stepping over things just to get by. Make room in the aisles for them so they'll have easy access to the products and to the rest of the shop.

Some of these suggestions can be implemented for the internet as well. Conduct a survey or ask some of your customers what positive changes they think you can. You may be surprised with the answers. It's very important that you tune in to the customer's needs.

How to Get a Feng Shui Consultant

If you need the services of a Feng Shui consultant, research very carefully and thoroughly. You can always get more information online and take it from there. Write down everything that you want from your consultant. There are also some schools where Feng Shui is taught. Let whoever you speak to know exactly what you're looking for and what you would like to achieve. You can check them out and make a decision to see who would be best for your needs. Remember that there is never any rush.

Feel free to contact us at anytime at:www.lightwakers.com. We can provide assistance and we do offer a full Feng Shui design and consulting service too.

'Shift your energy, not just your furniture. As by doing this you will transform how you live, work and play.'

Please never forget:

'Every day you move mountains, touch lives and perform miracles. Everyday you're a success, someone's hero and an example. Everyday... You change the world.'

Conclusion

Whether it's to improve your health, love life or finances, Feng Shui has been incorporated as a way to do this. The method has worked for the Chinese people for many years. Since it has spread, people are curious to find out how it can help them. This e-book has provided plenty of information to get you started on your journey to abundance and other things that can enhance your life. However, I have only briefly touched on this diverse and very deep ancient art.

If you stay on the right path with this and you are serious about making significant changes in your life, **you will** see a difference. **You will** be amazed at how much healthier you've become. You will be so excited to get intimate with your partner and it'll be breathtaking! With your finances, **you will** have more money than you ever dreamed possible! Just remember that everything won't happen overnight and that it will take time before you see a change in your life for the better. Stick with it, stay positive and watch as your life unfolds for the better.

Good luck on your journey. Stay in touch. We love hearing back from anyone who we have crossed paths with, regardless of when, where or how.

Facebook: www.facebook.com/LightWakers

Instagram: @light_wakers

Author's Instagram: @rob_horrocks

Twitter: @lightwakers001

Author's Twitter: @Rob_Horrocks1

Bagua Map

WEALTH, PROSPERITY AND SELF-WORTH	FAME, REPUTATION & SOCIAL LIFE	MARRIAGE, RELATIONSHIPS AND PARTNERSHIPS
ELEMENT: WOOD *SOUTHEAST* LATE SPRING **COLORS:** PURPLE, GREEN, GOLD	**ELEMENT:** FIRE *SOUTH* EARLY SUMMER **COLORS:** RED, BRIGHT ORANGE	**ELEMENT:** EARTH *SOUTHWEST* LATE SUMMER **COLORS:** PINK, SKIN TONES, EARTH TONES
HEALTH, FAMILY AND COMMUNITY	GOOD FORTUNE CENTER	CHILDREN, CREATIVITY & ENTERTAINMENT
ELEMENT: WOOD *EAST* EARLY SPRING **COLORS:** GREEN	**ELEMENT:** EARTH *HEART CENTER* **COLORS:** YELLOW, EARTH TONES	**ELEMENT:** METAL *WEST* EARLY FALL **COLORS:** WHITE, BRIGHT AND PASTEL COLORS
WISDOM, SELF-KNOWLEDGE AND REST	CAREER, LIFE MISSION & INDIVIDUALITY	HELPFUL PEOPLE, SPIRITUAL LIFE & TRAVEL
ELEMENT: EARTH *NORTHEAST* LATE WINTER, **COLORS:** BLUE-GREEN	**ELEMENT:** WATER *NORTH* EARLY WINTER **COLORS:** DARK BLUE, BLACK	**ELEMENT:** METAL *NORTHWEST* LATE FALL, **COLORS:** GRAY, MAUVE

WALL THAT CONTAINS THE MAIN ENTRANCE

Printed in Great Britain
by Amazon

35637174R00033